USDA United States
Department
of Agriculture

Forest Service

**Rocky Mountain
Research Station**

Resource Bulletin
RMRS-RB-9

August 2009

Wyoming's Forest Products Industry and Timber Harvest, 2005

Jason P. Brandt, Todd A. Morgan, and Mike T. Thompson

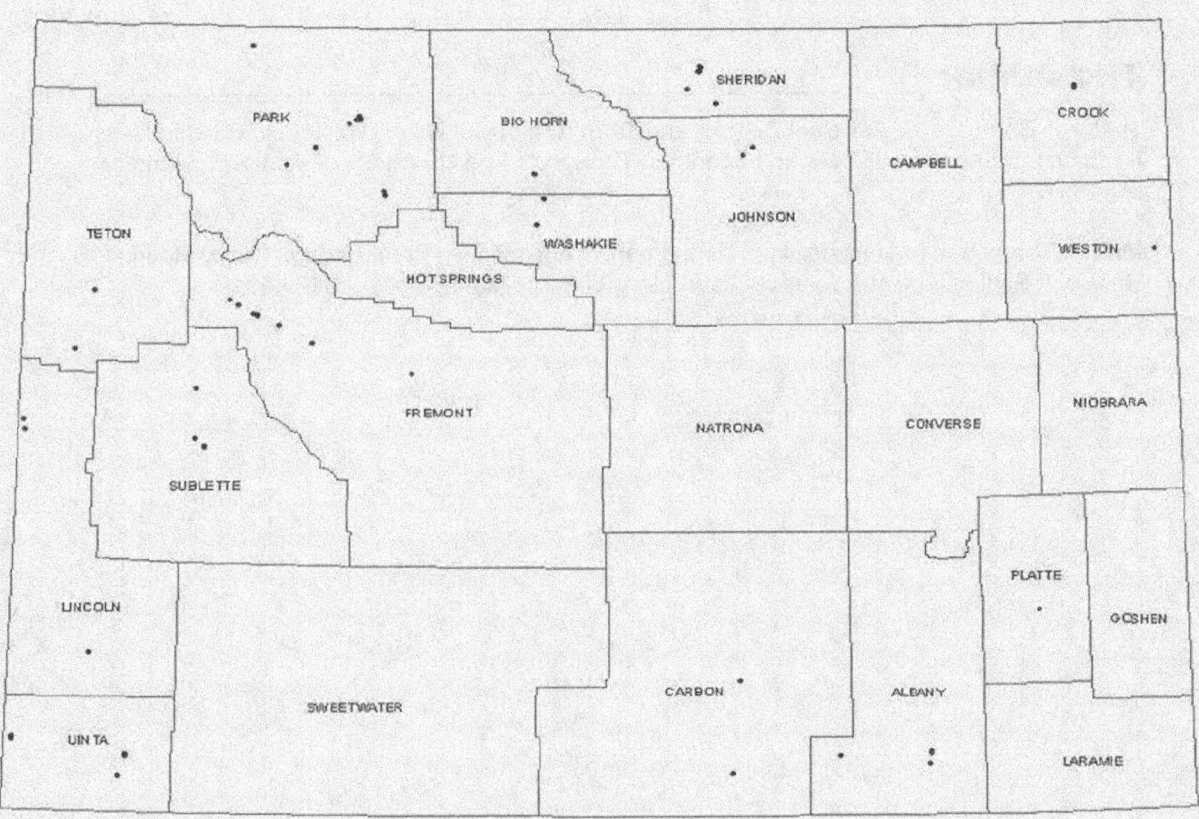

Abstract

This report traces the flow of Wyoming's 2005 timber harvest through the primary timber-processing industry to the wholesale market and residue-using sectors. The structure, capacity, operations, and conditions of Wyoming's primary forest products industry are described; and volumes and uses of wood fiber are quantified. Historical and recent changes in Wyoming's forest products industry, including harvest, production, and sales are also discussed.

Keywords: capacity, lumber production, mill residue, overrun, sawtimber volume

The Author

Jason P. Brandt is the Assistant Director and **Todd A. Morgan** is the Director of Forest Industry Research, Bureau of Business and Economic Research, The University of Montana, Missoula, MT 59812.

Mike T. Thompson is a forester, U.S. Department of Agriculture, Forest Service, Rocky Mountain Research Station, Forestry Sciences Laboratory, 507 25th Street, Ogden, UT 84401.

Report Highlights _____

- A total of 59 primary wood-processing facilities operated in 15 Wyoming counties during 2005. These facilities included 21 sawmills, 18 log home manufacturers, 8 log furniture manufacturers, 8 post and pole producers, and 4 other wood products facilities.

- Wyoming's total estimated capacity to process timber in 2005 was 132 million board feet (MMBF) Scribner. Wyoming's wood processing facilities used about 67 percent of processing capacity in 2005, processing almost 89 MMBF of timber.

- Sales value of Wyoming's primary forest products in 2005 was nearly $76 million free on board (f.o.b.) the producing mill. Lumber and sawn products accounted for nearly $59 million, and log home sales exceeded $9 million.

- Wyoming's 2005 timber harvest volume was 64 MMBF, with 66 percent of the timber coming from private timberlands, 28 percent from national forests, 4 percent from state-owned lands, and slightly more than 1 percent from the BLM.

- Ponderosa pine (*Pinus ponderosa*) was Wyoming's most harvested species in 2005, accounting for 44.2 MMBF, or 69 percent of the total harvest, followed by lodgepole pine (*Pinus contorta*) with 15.4 percent or 9.9 MMBF.

- Wyoming's timber harvest (64 MMBF) and volume processed (87 MMBF) are quite different because of the substantial timber flow into and out of the state. Nearly 60 percent of the timber processed in Wyoming during 2005 came from outside the state, while more than 40 percent of Wyoming's harvest was processed outside the state.

- Wyoming mills relied heavily on out-of-state timber from both public and private lands in 2005. Two-thirds of public lands timber processed in Wyoming came from outside the state, while half of the private timber received by Wyoming mills came from outside the state.

- Wyoming timber processors generated about 126,000 bone dry units (BDU) of residue in 2005. About 99 percent of both coarse and fine residues were utilized; however, almost a third of the bark was not used.

Contents_____

Wyoming's Forest Products Industry and Timber Harvest, 2005

Jason P. Brandt
Todd A. Morgan
Mike T. Thompson

Introduction

This report focuses on the results of a statewide census of Wyoming's primary forest products industry for calendar year 2005. The report includes discussion of trends since 2000, as well as longer-term historic trends drawn from other sources. The report's principal goals are to determine the utilization of Wyoming's timber harvest, identify the type and number of primary forest products firms operating in 2005 and their sources of raw material, and quantify outputs of finished products. Data on subsequent years are provided where available.

The University of Montana's Bureau of Business and Economic Research (BBER) and the USDA, Forest Service, Rocky Mountain Research Station (Ogden, Utah) cooperated in the analysis and preparation of this report. BBER, in cooperation with the Forest Inventory and Analysis (FIA) programs at the Rocky Mountain and Pacific Northwest Research Stations, has developed a system to collect, compile, and make available state and county information on the operations of the forest products industry—the Forest Industries Data Collection System (FIDACS).

Forest Industries Data Collection System

This effort is the third application of FIDACS in Wyoming; the first was in 1976 (Keegan et al. 1979), with the second in 2000 (Morgan et al. 2005). The system is based on a census of primary forest product manufacturers located in a given state and facilities in surrounding states that receive timber harvested from the state of interest. Primary forest product manufacturers are firms that process timber into manufactured products such as lumber, and facilities like wood pellet plants, that use the wood fiber residue directly from timber processors. Wyoming's primary forest products manufacturers were identified through telephone directories, directories of the forest products industries (Random Lengths 2006; RISI 2007), and with the assistance of the manufacturers themselves. Through a written questionnaire or telephone interview, manufacturers provided the following detailed information for each facility operating during calendar year 2005:

- plant location, production capacity, and employment
- volume of raw material received, by county and ownership
- species of timber received and live/dead proportions
- preferred and accepted log lengths and diameters
- finished product volumes, types, sales value, and market locations
- utilization and marketing of manufacturing residue

Firms cooperating in the 2005 Wyoming census processed virtually all of the state's commercial timber harvest. Volumes and characteristics of Wyoming timber processed by out-of-state firms were determined by surveying facilities in nearby states. A variety of publications and information provided by federal, state, and industry managers were

USDA Forest Service Resour. Bull. RMRS-RB-9. 2009

1

used to verify estimates of Wyoming's total timber harvest and wood products production and sales.

Information collected through FIDACS is stored at the University of Montana's Bureau of Business and Economic Research. Additional information is available by request. However, individual, firm-level data are confidential and cannot be released.

Historical Overview of Wyoming's Forest Products Industry

Wyoming's forest products industry expanded dramatically after the Second World War through the 1960s, in response to a strong demand for lumber and other wood products coupled with ready availability of federal timber. From the late 1940s to the late 1960s, Wyoming's lumber production increased more than threefold fueled by the state's timber harvest more than doubling during that time period. Through the 1970s demand for wood products remained high, the lumber markets were strong, and Wyoming's production remained high with housing starts in the U.S. exceeding 2 million units for five of the years in the decade.

Late in 1979 the demand for wood products and strong lumber markets came to an abrupt end with the precipitous drop in the U.S. housing and construction industries brought on by historically high interest rates. The sharp increase in interest rates led the U.S. and Wyoming's forest products industry into a 6-year period with the poorest sustained markets since the Great Depression. The resulting recession of 1980 only became more severe through 1982. By 1983 conditions had improved in the U.S. housing and construction industries resulting in increased demand and very high levels of forest products consumption in the United States through 1985. However, even with high demand and consumption in the United States, wood product prices remained low due to a high-valued U.S. dollar, which in turn led to decreased U.S. exports and increased Canadian imports.

Forest products markets really began to improve during the last half of the 1980s. A lower-value U.S. dollar and strong economy led to the increasing prices for wood products and Wyoming's industry responded with record production. The record production occurred because mills had considerable timber under contract from the early 1980s, which they had delayed harvesting during the poor market period. Mills experienced a temporary abundance of timber from national forests in the late 1980s when they were required to harvest some of the timber to fulfill contract obligations.

During the 1990s, the forest products industry in Wyoming and throughout the western United States was impacted by sharply reduced timber availability from federal lands. Across the United States, harvest from federal timberlands (mainly national forests) fell by more than 8 billion board feet, a decline of more than 80 percent. This precipitous drop in harvest levels resulted from numerous constraints on harvesting timber on public lands, including appeals and litigation of timber sales, threatened and endangered species protection, and cumulative impacts of past harvesting on other resources such as water quality and wildlife. This decrease in timber availability lead to the continued decline of the capacity to process timber in Wyoming where harvest from federal lands had historically provided over 75 percent (WWPA 1964-2006) of the timber processed. The harvest from federal lands throughout the West followed a similar downward trend throughout the 1990s, and timber-processing capacity was lost in Wyoming and other western states (Keegan et al. 2006).

In combination with the very large decreases in federal timber availability, changes in U.S. and global economies had a large influence on the industry. The first Gulf War led to a recession in 1990 and 1991, which brought about decreased lumber prices. The market had reverse course by 1993 when high demand drove lumber prices to near-record highs with more robust U.S. and global economies and the significant reductions in the federal timber supply nationwide. The markets remained strong during the last half of the 1990s, with the exception of a modest decline in the U.S. economy in 1995, and sharp declines in a number of Asian economies in late 1997 and 1998. Rising imports of Canadian softwood lumber became an increasingly contentious issue, leading, in 1996, to quotas on imports from the major timber producing provinces in Canada.

Improvement in the global economy and strengthening of the U.S. economy in 1999 improved the wood products market until 2000, when housing starts slipped in the United States and Japan. The September 11th terrorist attacks only worsened the U.S. and global recession in 2001. The reduction in housing starts brought about low lumber prices through the first half of 2003 (WWPA 1964-2006). Even with record U.S. lumber consumption of more than 56 billion board feet in 2002 and the replacement of the quota on Canadian softwood lumber in 2001 with a 27 percent duty, the low lumber prices continued. The persistent low prices were a result of poor economic conditions throughout much of the world and an excess lumber supply in the U.S. market.

During the second half of 2003, prices for wood products began to experience a boost due to the increased domestic and global demand for wood products, a weakening U.S. dollar, and a countervailing duty on softwood lumber imported into the United States from Canada. This trend carried through 2004 and 2005, with prices reaching near record levels due in part to a very strong U.S. housing market and a robust global demand for wood products. By 2006, prices for most wood products experienced a precipitous decline as the U.S. housing market slowed dramatically. High fuel prices increased logging and transportation costs. Influenced by wood products markets, fuel prices, and timber availability, Wyoming's forest products industry suffered additional losses in 2006 and 2007, with the permanent closure of two of Wyoming's larger sawmills further reducing timber-processing capacity in the state.

Wyoming's Timber Harvest, Products, and Flow

This section focuses on ownership and geographic sources of timber, types of timber products harvested and processed, species composition, and movement of timber. It examines Wyoming's timber harvest and the industry's use of timber in the direct manufacture of products during 2005 and makes comparisons with previous years. Timber harvested for residential fuelwood is not included.

Wyoming has approximately 6.5 million acres of "nonreserved timberland" that are available for timber harvest (Thompson et al. 2005). Nonreserved timberland includes land that is "not permanently reserved from wood products utilization through statute or administrative designation" (Bechtold and Patterson 2005). Examples of reserved lands include National Forest Wilderness areas and National Parks and Monuments. The USDA Forest Service's National Forest System manages the largest portion of Wyoming's nonreserved timberland, with responsibility for 62 percent or 4.0 million acres. The second largest ownership class is non-industrial private forest (NIPF) land, including tribal lands, which account for 23 percent of timberland, or approximately 1.5 million acres. Other public owners maintain the remaining 15 percent, or just under 1.0 million acres, of Wyoming's nonreserved timberland. Other public lands include timberland managed by the State of Wyoming, Bureau of Land Management (BLM), and county and municipal governments.

Available sawtimber volume on Wyoming's nonreserved timberland is approximately 37.3 billion board feet Scribner (Thompson et al. 2005). Approximately 80 percent (29.9 billion board feet) of this volume is on National Forest land, while 13 percent (4.8 billion board feet) is located on non-industrial private forests, and the remaining 7 percent (2.6 billion board feet) on other public lands. Approximately 26 percent of the sawtimber volume is comprised of Engelmann spruce (*Picea engelmannii* Parry ex Engelm.), 23 percent is lodgepole pine (*Pinus contorta* Dougl. ex Loud. var. *latifolia* Engelm.),

16 percent Douglas-fir (*Pseudotsuga menziesii* (Mirb.) Franco), 13 percent subalpine fir (*Abies lasiocarpa* (Hook.) Nutt.), and 10 percent ponderosa pine (*Pinus ponderosa* Dougl. ex Laws.). Net annual growth of sawtimber on nonreserved timberland is approximately 639 million board feet (MMBF) per year. Lodgepole pine accounts for nearly 33 percent of net growth, followed by Engelmann spruce (21 percent), and ponderosa pine (17 percent).

In 2005, timber harvested from Wyoming and manufactured into wood products came from four land ownership categories: nonindustrial private lands, national forests, BLM, and state-owned lands. Wyoming has no large tracts of timberland owned by individuals or companies operating primary wood processing plants.

The 2005 harvest volume, at 13.7 MMCF or 64.0 MMBF Scribner, was about 10 percent lower than the 2000 harvest of 70.5 MMBF (Morgan et al. 2005). Since the mid-1990s, harvest volume has averaged about half of what it was during the 1960s through 1980s (fig. 1). The ownership sources for the majority and minority portions of the harvest are also quite different in more recent years than historically. For example, in 1976, approximately 147 MMBF of timber were harvested in Wyoming; public lands provided 78 percent of the harvest, and private lands provided 22 percent (Keegan and White 1979). In 2000, private lands accounted for 73 percent of the harvest, and in 2005, 66 percent of the timber harvested in Wyoming came from private timberlands, while national forests accounted for less than 30 percent, state-owned lands produced 4 percent, and just over 1 percent came from BLM lands (table 1).

Approximately 80 percent of Wyoming's 2005 timber harvest came from five counties. Crook County was the source of 58 percent of the timber harvest, while Park County contributed 10 percent. Big Horn, Johnson, and Sheridan counties each contributed 4 percent (table 2). Crook County likewise led the state's timber harvest during 2000, providing 45 percent of Wyoming's timber harvest (Morgan et al. 2005).

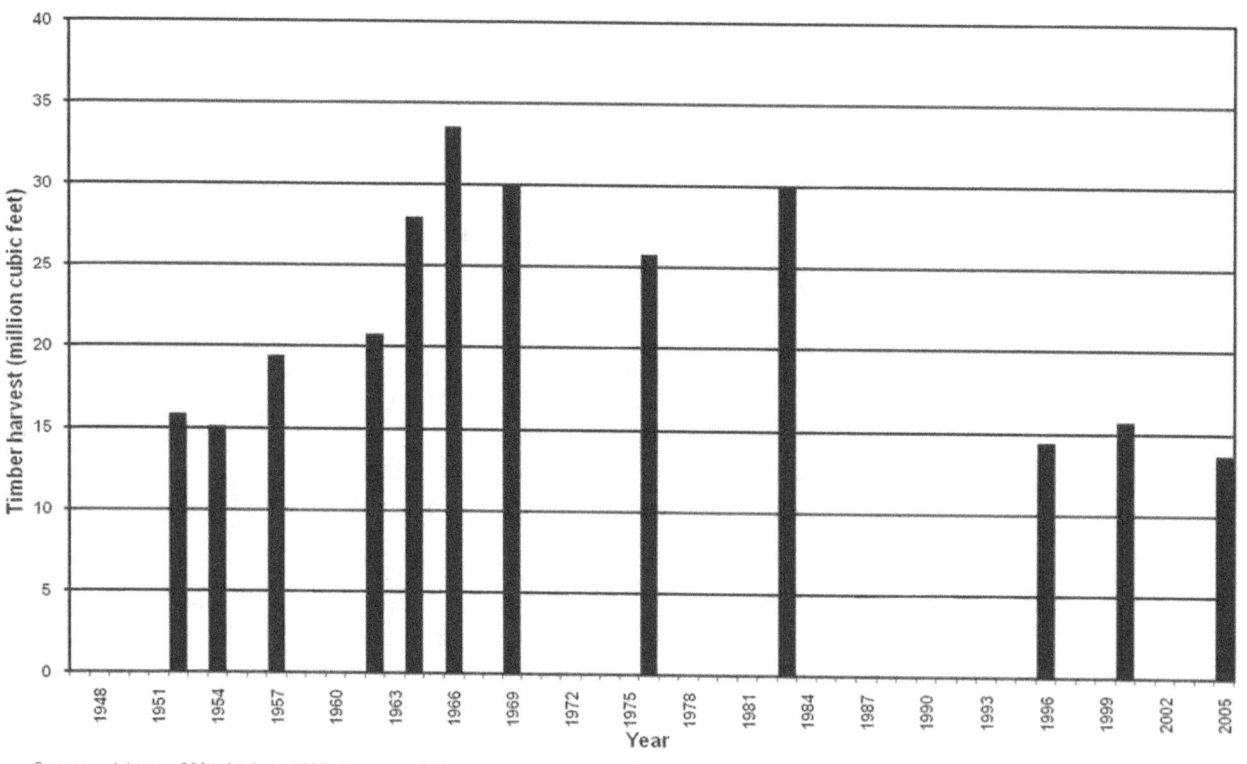

Sources: Johnson 2001, McLain 1987, Keegan and White 1979, Setzer 1971, Setzer and Wilson 1970, Spencer and Farrenkopf 1964.

Figure 1—Wyoming timber harvest, 1947-2005.

USDA Forest Service Resour. Bull. RMRS-RB-9. 2009

Table 1—Wyoming's 2005 timber harvest by ownership source.

Ownership	Harvest	Percent of total
	MBF[a]	
Industrial	—	—
Nonindustrial private and Tribal	42,380	66.2
National Forest	18,189	28.4
Bureau of Land Management	903	1.4
State	2,565	4.0
Total	64,037	100

[a] Harvest volume expressed in thousand board feet (MBF) Scribner.

Table 2—Wyoming's 2005 timber harvest by county and ownership class.

Resource area / county	National Forest	Private and Tribal	Other[a] public	Total	Percentage of total
	--------------------- MBF[b] ---------------------				
Northeast					
Campbell	—	1,205	—	1,205	2
Crook	8,209	28,722	237	37,168	58
Weston	20	603	—	623	1
Northeast total	8,229	30,529	237	38,995	61
North Central					
Big Horn	704	1,540	214	2,458	4
Johnson	700	1,504	350	2,554	4
Sheridan	2,300	14	—	2,314	4
Washakie	—	1,917	37	1,954	3
North Central total	3,704	4,975	601	9,281	14
Northwest					
Fremont	1,041	562	160	1,763	3
Hot Springs	—	—	3	3	0
Lincoln	120	325	550	995	2
Park	3,527	1,150	1,512	6,189	10
Sublette	3	20	—	23	0
Teton	27	15	—	42	0
Northwest total	4,718	2,072	2,225	9,015	14
Southeast					
Albany	1,506	—	—	1,506	2
Carbon	—	39	5	44	0
Converse	—	974	—	974	2
Goshen	—	—	—	—	0
Laramie	—	—	—	—	0
Natrona	32	1,221	400	1,653	3
Niobrara	—	—	—	—	0
Platte	—	—	—	—	0
Southeast total	1,538	2,234	405	4,176	7
Southwest					
Sweetwater	—	—	—	—	0
Uinta	—	2,570	—	2,570	4
Southwest total	—	2,570	—	2,570	4
Wyoming total	18,189	42,380	3,468	64,037	100

[a] Other public ownership includes BLM and state lands.
[b] Harvest volume expressed in thousand board feet (MBF) Scribner.

USDA Forest Service Resour. Bull. RMRS-RB-9. 2009

5

As in previous years, ponderosa pine and lodgepole pine were Wyoming's most harvested species (table 3). Ponderosa pine accounted for 44.2 MMBF, or 69.0 percent of the total harvest in 2005, followed by lodgepole pine with 15.4 percent or 9.9 MMBF. The remaining harvest was Douglas-fir with 9.0 percent, Engelmann spruce and Black Hills (white) spruce (*Picea glauca* (Moench) Voss) with 5.7 percent, true firs (*Abies* spp.) with just under 1.0 percent, and other softwoods and hardwoods accounting for 0.02 percent of the harvest.

Harvest by Product Type

Wyoming's timber harvest falls into three general product categories: saw logs—timber sawn to produce lumber, mine timbers, and the like; house logs—timber used to manufacture log homes; and other products—timber used to manufacture posts, poles, log furniture, and other roundwood products.

Saw logs were the primary timber product harvested in Wyoming in 2005, accounting for 94 percent (60.4 MMBF) of the total harvest (table 4). House logs comprised less than 1 percent of the 2005 harvest, while other products accounted for about 5 percent (3.1 MMBF). The product shares differed little from previous years (McLain 1987).

Table 3—Wyoming's timber harvest by species for various years.

Species	1983	2000	2005
	Thousand board feet (MBF), Scribner		
Ponderosa pine	70,203	42,121	44,156
Lodgepole pine	60,058	18,824	9,853
Douglas-fir	4,688	3,562	5,785
True firs	2,492	1,661	597
Engelmann/Black Hills spruce	9,528	4,112	3,640
Other softwoods	93	13	4
Hardwoods	36	201	3
All species	147,098	70,494	64,037
	- - - - - - - *Percent of harvest* - - - - - - -		
Ponderosa pine	47.7	59.8	69.0
Lodgepole pine	40.8	26.7	15.4
Douglas-fir	3.2	5.1	9.0
True firs	1.7	2.4	0.9
Engelmann/Black Hills spruce	6.5	5.8	5.7
Other species	0.1	0.0	0.0
All species	100.0	100.0	100.0

Sources: McLain 1987 and Morgan et al. 2005.

Table 4—Wyoming's 2005 timber harvest volume by ownership source and product type.

Ownership source	Saw logs	House logs	Other products[a]	All products
	- *MBF*[b] -			
Private timberlands:	40,333	211	1,836	42,380
Industrial	—	—	—	—
Nonindustrial and Tribal	40,333	211	1,836	42,380
Public timberlands:	20,078	344	1,236	21,657
National Forests	17,108	339	742	18,189
Other public	2,969	5	494	3,468
Total	60,411	555	3,072	64,037

[a] Other products include logs for posts, poles, and other roundwood products.
[b] Harvest volume expressed in thousand board feet (MBF) Scribner.

In 1976, saw logs comprised 91 percent of Wyoming's industrial timber harvest (Keegan and White 1979), and house logs together with "other products" accounted for just over 2 percent of the harvest. The remaining 7 percent of Wyoming's 1976 timber harvest was made up of roundwood pulpwood. In 2000, saw logs accounted for 89 percent of Wyoming's industrial timber harvest (Morgan et al. 2005), house logs comprised less than 3 percent, and other products made up about 8 percent of Wyoming's timber harvest.

Private timberlands supplied 67 percent (40.3 MMBF) of Wyoming's 2005 saw log harvest, while national forest timberlands made up 28 percent (17.1 MMBF), with other public timberlands supplying the remaining 5 percent (3.0 MMBF). In 2000, private timberlands provided a slightly larger proportion of saw log harvest, providing 73 percent (46 MMBF), while saw logs from Wyoming's national forest timberlands made up a lower proportion, providing only 20 percent or 12.8 MMBF, and the remaining 7 percent of saw log harvest was from other public timberlands (Morgan et al. 2005). National forest timberlands were the primary source of Wyoming's house log harvest, providing 61 percent (0.3 MMBF) in 2005. Private timberlands supplied 38 percent (0.2 MMBF), and other public lands (State and BLM) supplied the remaining 1 percent of Wyoming's 2005 house log harvest. During 2000, other public timberlands provided 54 percent (1.0 MMBF) of Wyoming's house log harvest, national forests provided an additional 0.8 MMBF (43 percent), and the remaining 3 percent came from private timberlands (Morgan et al. 2005). Sixty percent of Wyoming's 3.1 MMBF harvest for other materials came from private ownerships, while the remaining 40 percent was split between national forest and other public lands providing 24 and 16 percent, respectively. In 2000, 91 percent (5.2 MMBF) of Wyoming's timber harvest for other products was from private timberlands, while the remaining 9 percent (0.5 MMBF) came from other public timberlands (5 percent) and national forest timberlands (4 percent) (Morgan et al. 2005).

Harvest by Geographic Source

The geographic source of Wyoming's timber harvest has been from the mountainous regions of the state, where sufficient moisture allows timber to achieve a merchantable size (Green and Conner 1989). Wyoming's timber harvest was divided among five resource areas for 2005: northeast, north central, northwest, southeast, and southwest. The Northeast Resource Area includes Campbell, Crook, and Weston Counties and accounted for 61 percent (39 MMBF) of Wyoming's 2005 timber harvest (table 2). The North Central Resource Area includes Big Horn, Johnson, Sheridan, and Washakie Counties and was responsible for providing 14 percent (9.3 MMBF) of Wyoming's timber harvest. The Northwest Resource Area also provided 14 percent (9.0 MMBF) and includes Fremont, Hot Springs, Lincoln, Park, Sublette, and Teton Counties. Seven percent (4.2 MMBF) of the harvest originated in the Southeast Resource Area, which includes the counties of Albany, Carbon, Converse, Goshen, Laramie, Natrona, Niobrara, and Platte. The southwest resource area accounted for 4 percent (2.6 MMBF) and includes Sweetwater and Uinta counties.

Previous reports by Keegan and White (1979) and Morgan et al. (2005) summarized Wyoming's 1976 and 2000 saw log harvest by three geographic regions: west, northeast, and southeast. The west region included Fremont, Hot Springs, Lincoln, Park, Sublette, Sweetwater, Teton, and Uinta counties. In 1976 these areas accounted for 38 percent of Wyoming's saw log harvest; by 2000 the proportion had dropped to only 12 percent, and in 2005 this region provided just under 18 percent of Wyoming's saw log harvest. The northeast region included Big Horn, Campbell, Crook, Johnson, Sheridan, Washakie, and Weston counties. These counties were responsible for 35 percent of the saw log harvest in 1976. By 2000 this percentage had doubled to 70 percent, and by 2005 these counties provided close to 75 percent of Wyoming's saw log harvest. The southeast region,

USDA Forest Service Resour. Bull. RMRS-RB-9. 2009

7

comprised of Albany, Carbon, Converse, Goshen, Laramie, Natrona, Niobrara, and Platte Counties, yielded 27 percent of Wyoming's 1976 saw log harvest, compared to 18 percent in 2000 and only 7 percent in 2005. Shifts in the volume and proportions of timber harvested among the three geographic regions are closely tied to decreases in national forest harvest and changes in private landowner management activities.

Harvest by Species

The species composition of Wyoming's saw log harvest has shifted from predominantly lodgepole pine (73 percent in 1969) with substantial components of ponderosa pine and Engelmann spruce to a largely ponderosa pine (73 percent in 2005) harvest with decreasing proportions of lodgepole pine and spruce (table 5). The proportion of Douglas-fir in the saw log harvest has increased from just under 3 percent in 1969 to slightly over 9 percent in 2005. The proportion of spruce in the saw log harvest decreased from nearly 12 percent in 1969 to 6 percent in 2005. True firs also decreased slightly from just below 3 percent to only 1 percent. This species shift corresponds to the ongoing geographic shift in harvest from western counties, where lodgepole pine, spruce, and Douglas-fir are the predominant timber species, to northeastern counties where ponderosa pine is the predominant species. Furthermore, nearly 88 percent of Wyoming's lodgepole pine volume on nonreserved timberland occurs on National Forest System (NFS) land and the reduction in timber harvest on NFS lands equates to a reduction in harvest of lodgepole pine in Wyoming (Thompson et al. 2005).

In 2005, lodgepole pine accounted for 73 percent of volume harvested for house log production, which is a slight decrease from 2000 when lodgepole pine accounted for 86 percent of the volume harvested for house log production. Douglas-fir experienced the largest increase in proportion of volume harvested for house log production, accounting for 21 percent in 2005 versus less than 1 percent in 2000 (table 6). Spruce, ponderosa pine, and true firs collectively accounted for the remaining 6 percent. Lodgepole pine, at 91 percent, was also the most common species harvested for other primary wood products in 2005. Spruce was second at almost 9 percent, with Douglas-fir, other softwoods, hardwoods, and true firs combined making up less than 1 percent.

Table 5—Species composition of Wyoming's historical saw log harvest.

Species	1962	1969	1976	1983	2000	2005
	- - - - - - - - - - - - - - - - - Thousand cubic feet - - - - - - - - - - - - - - - - -					
Ponderosa pine	3,735	3,383	6,000	14,138	8,870	9,235
Lodgepole pine	11,460	21,300	12,546	11,990	2,869	1,394
Douglas-fir	931	833	1,323	937	622	1,183
True firs	516	369	1,084	503	222	124
Engelmann/Black Hills spruce	2,970	3,399	2,563	1,902	863	761
Other species	5	3	75	26	3	0
All species	19,617	29,287	23,591	29,496	13,449	12,697
	Percent of harvest					
Species	1962	1969	1976	1983	2000	2005
Ponderosa pine	19.0	11.6	25.4	47.9	66.0	72.7
Lodgepole pine	58.4	72.7	53.2	40.6	21.3	11.0
Douglas-fir	4.7	2.8	5.6	3.2	4.6	9.3
True firs	2.6	1.3	4.6	1.7	1.6	1.0
Engelmann/Black Hills spruce	15.1	11.6	10.9	6.4	6.4	6.0
Other species	0.0	0.0	0.3	0.1	0.0	0.0
All species	100	100	100	100	100	100

Sources: Keegan and White 1979; Keegan et al. 1979; McLain 1987; Morgan et al. 2005; Setzer 1971; Spencer and Farrenkopf 1964.

Table 6—Wyoming's timber harvest volume by species and product type, 2005.

Species	Saw logs	House logs	Other products [a]	All products
			MBF [b]	
Douglas-fir	5,654	115	16	5,785
True firs	593	3	1	597
Ponderosa pine	44,142	14	—	44,156
Lodgepole pine	6,662	407	2,784	9,853
Spruce	3,361	15	264	3,640
Other softwoods	1	—	3	4
Hardwoods	—	—	3	3
All species	60,411	555	3,072	64,037

[a] Other products include logs for posts, poles, and other roundwood products.
[b] Harvest volume expressed in thousand board feet (MBF) Scr bner.

Timber Flow

Wyoming has proportionately larger log flows into and out of the state than any of the western states. Wyoming imported 49.9 MMBF of timber from other states and exported 27.4 MMBF, making Wyoming a net importer of 22.5 MMBF of timber in 2005 (table 7). Consequently, more than 77 MMBF of timber crossed Wyoming state lines in 2005, a volume equivalent to 121 percent of the timber harvested and 89 percent of the volume processed in the state during the year. During 2000, more than 87 MMBF crossed Wyoming's state line, however Wyoming imported more timber (65 MMBF) from other states and exported less (22.4 MMBF) timber than in 2005 (Morgan et al. 2005). However, when you look at the amount of timber crossing Wyoming's state line for both years as a proportion of the timber harvest they are very similar with a volume equivalent of 124 percent in 2000 and 121 percent in 2005. Facilities in the North Central and Northeast Resource Area received the most out-of-state timber, nearly 28 MMBF followed by the Southeast Resource Area receiving nearly 16 MMBF (table 8). Mills in the Southwest Resource Area received just over 5.5 MMBF from out-of-state and the Northwest Resource Area received less than 1 MMBF. The Northeast Resource Area shipped the most timber out-of-state, with just over 24 MMBF going to facilities in other states. The Northwest Resource Area shipped more than 3 MMBF of timber to facilities outside of Wyoming, while the Southeast and Southwest Resource areas combined shipped only 75 MBF to plants in other states.

Table 7—Wyoming's 2005 timber imports and exports to other states.

Timber products	Imports	Exports	Net imports
		MBF [a]	
Saw logs	47,073	27,288	19,785
House logs	1,561	16	1,545
Other [b]	1,259	140	1,119
Total products	49,893	27,444	22,450

[a] Volume expressed in thousand board feet (MBF) Scr bner.
[b] Other products include logs for posts, poles, and other roundwood products.

USDA Forest Service Resour. Bull. RMRS-RB-9. 2009

9

Table 8—Wyoming's timber flow by resource area, 2005.

Destination (resource area)	Geographic source of timber					Total timber received in Wyoming
	North Central and Northeast[a]	Northwest[b]	Southeast[c]	Southwest[d]	Out-of-State	
	Thousand board feet, Scribner (MBF)					
North Central and Northeast[a]	23,991.9	591.0	422.0	—	27,952.8	52,957.7
Northwest[b]	6.0	4,532.8	—	—	661.5	5,200.3
Southeast[c]	-	-	2,149.4	—	15,726.0	17,875.4
Southwest[d]	-	800.0	1,600.0	2,500.0	5,553.0	10,453.0
Shipped out of Wyoming	24,277.8	3,091.0	5.0	70.0		86,486.4
					Wyoming's timber harvest	
Total Wyoming timber harvest by resource area	48,275.7	9,014.8	4,176.4	2,570.0	64,036.9	

[a] North Central and Northeast resource areas are combined to avoid disclosure of firm level data. Counties include: Big Horn, Campbell, Crook, Johnson, Sheridan, Washakie, and Weston.
[b] Northwest resource area counties include: Fremont, Hot Springs, Lincoln, Park, Sublette, and Teton.
[c] Southeast resource area counties include: A bany, Carbon, Converse, Goshen, Laramie, Natrona, Niobrara, and Platte.
[d] Southwest resource area counties include: Sweetwater and Uinta.

The largest volume of timber imported by Wyoming mills came from Colorado, followed by South Dakota and Montana. These three states combined were responsible for 87 percent (43.3 MMBF) of the timber imported into Wyoming. In 2000, these three states supplied 86 percent (55.9 MMBF) of the timber imported into Wyoming with South Dakota being the origin of the largest volume (Morgan et al. 2005). The remaining 13 percent came from Utah, Idaho, Nebraska, Washington, and Canada. Just over 40 percent (27.4 MMBF) of Wyoming's timber harvest went to other states for processing, with South Dakota receiving more than 80 percent (22.85 MMBF) of the exported timber and the remainder going to Montana and Utah. During 2000, Idaho, Montana, and South Dakota received about 32 percent (22.4 MMBF) of Wyoming's timber harvest, with South Dakota receiving over 80 percent of the exported volume (Morgan et al. 2005).

Timber harvested and processed within Wyoming generally did not move long distances. In 2005, 67 percent of the timber harvested and processed in Wyoming was processed in the county of harvest; another 24 percent was processed in an adjacent Wyoming county. Likewise, most out-of-state timber processed by Wyoming mills came from adjacent, although out-of-state, counties.

Timber Use by Wyoming Mills

The volume of timber processed in Wyoming (87 MMBF) is substantially larger than the timber harvest in the state (64 MMBF) because of the considerable timber flow into and out of the state. 49.9 MMBF Scribner of timber or 58 percent of the timber processed in Wyoming in 2005 came from outside the state. 27.4 MMBF Scribner or 43 percent of Wyoming's 2005 timber harvest was processed by facilities in other states. Private timberlands contributed 57 percent (49.4 MMBF) of the 86.5 MMBF timber processed in Wyoming mills in 2005 (table 9), public timberlands supplied just over 42 percent, and imports from Canada contributed about 1 percent.

Wyoming mills relied heavily on out-of-state timber from both public and private lands in 2005. Nearly 25.2 MMBF (69 percent) of the 36.4 MMBF of public lands timber processed in Wyoming came from outside the state, while about 24.5 MMBF (50 percent) of private timber received by Wyoming mills came from outside the state. The distribution of Wyoming's mills near the state's borders with national forests in South Dakota, Colorado, and Montana contributed to the large proportion of out-of-state public lands timber processed by Wyoming mills.

Table 9—Ownership source of timber delivered to Wyoming timber processing facilities, 2005.

Ownership source	Volume	Percent of total
	MBF [a]	
Private timberlands:	49,424	57.1
Industrial [b]	75	0.1
Nonindustrial	44,321	51.2
Tribal	5,028	5.8
Public timberlands:	36,862	42.6
National Forests	30,796	35.6
Other public	6,065	7.0
Canadian	201	0.2
Total	86,486	100

[a] Volume expressed in thousand board feet (MBF) Scr bner.
[b] Includes shipments of timber from other mills and out-of-state industrial timberlands.

USDA Forest Service Resour. Bull. RMRS-RB-9. 2009

11

Private lands contributed 58 percent (46.5 MMBF) of sawtimber receipts, with public lands contributing the remaining 42 percent (table 10). Public lands were the source of 71 percent of timber used for house logs and log homes, with only 19 percent originating from private lands, and 10 percent (200 MBF, Scribner) of house logs coming from Canada. In 2000, 12 percent (363 MBF, Scribner) of house logs processed in Wyoming were imported from Canada. Among mills utilizing timber for other products, private lands provided 60 percent of the timber used in 2005, public timberlands contributed just under 40 percent, and Canadian lands provided less than 1 percent.

Table 10—Ownership source of timber products delivered to Wyoming timber-processing facilities, 2005.

Ownership source	Saw logs	House logs	Other products [a]	All products
	---------------------- MBF [b] ----------------------			
Private timberlands:	46,504	399	2,521	49,424
Industrial [c]	—	75	—	75
Nonindustrial	41,544	300	2,477	44,321
Tribal	4,960	24	44	5,028
Public timberlands:	33,692	1,501	1,669	36,862
National Forests	28,126	1,496	1,175	30,796
Other public	5,566	5	494	6,065
Canadian	—	200	1	201
Total	80,196	2,100	4,191	86,487

[a] Other products include posts, poles, and other roundwood products.
[b] Volume expressed in thousand board feet (MBF) Scribner.
[c] Includes shipments of timber from other mills and out-of-state industrial timberlands.

Wyoming's Primary Forest Products Industry

The following section provides detail on Wyoming's forest products sectors that processed timber and mill residue into finished products during 2005: sawmills, house log and log home manufacturers, log furniture producers, and other primary wood products manufacturers.

The 2005 census identified 58 active primary forest products manufacturers in Wyoming. These plants produced an array of products including lumber and other sawn products, wood pellets, house logs, posts, poles, and log furniture (table 11). Sixty-two active firms were identified in the 1976 census (Keegan and White 1979), McLain (1987 and 1988) canvassed 41 firms in 1983, and Morgan et al. (2005) identified 55 firms operating in 2000. Most decreases in the number of firms have occurred in the sawmill sector, which had as many as 107 active sawmills in 1957 (Miller and Wilson 1959), 50 firms in 1976 (Keegan and White 1979), 23 active plants in 2000 (Morgan et al. 2005), and only 21 operating in 2005. In contrast, the number of primary wood products producers in other sectors has increased since 1976, including the addition of one post and pole facility, 14 house log manufacturers, three facilities producing fuel pellets, and 8 log furniture manufacturers (not reported in 1976).

In 2005, wood product manufacturing facilities operated in 15 of Wyoming's 23 counties (fig. 2), two fewer counties than in 1976 and one more county than in 2000. Park County contained 13 active timber-processing facilities, more than any other county, and three more than in 2000. Uinta County contained the second greatest number of facilities with eight, one less than in 2000. Only three other counties, Fremont, Sheridan, and Sublette had five or more facilities in 2005.

Table 11—Number of active Wyoming primary wood products facilities by county, 2005.

Resource area / county	Sawmills	Post and pole	House logs	Log furniture	Other [a]	Total
Northeast						
Campbell	—	—	—	—	—	—
Crook	2	—	—	—	—	2
Weston	1	—	—	—	—	1
Northeast total	3	—	—	—	—	3
North Central						
Big Horn	1	1	—	—	—	2
Johnson	1	—	—	—	—	1
Sheridan	1	—	3	1	1	6
Washakie	—	1	1	—	1	3
North Central total	3	2	4	1	2	12
Northwest						
Fremont	4	—	2	—	—	6
Hot Springs	—	—	—	—	—	—
Lincoln	1	—	1	—	—	2
Park	3	1	6	3	—	13
Sublette	1	1	2	1	—	5
Teton	—	—	—	2	—	2
Northwest total	9	2	11	6	—	28
Southeast						
Albany	1	1	1	—	1	4
Carbon	1	1	1	—	—	3
Converse	—	—	—	—	—	—
Goshen	—	—	—	—	—	—
Laramie	—	—	—	—	—	—
Natrona	—	—	—	—	—	—
Niobrara	—	—	—	—	—	—
Platte	1	—	—	—	—	1
Southeast total	3	2	2	—	1	8
Southwest						
Sweetwater	—	—	—	—	—	—
Uinta	3	2	1	1	1	8
Southwest total	3	2	1	1	1	8
All counties (2005)	21	8	18	8	4	**59**
2000 [b]	23	8	8	11	5	**55**
1983 [b]	34	3	4	—	—	**41**
1976 [b]	50	7	4	—	1	**62**
1962 [b]	76	—	—	—	—	**76**
1957 [b]	107	—	—	—	—	**107**

[a] Other facilities include firewood manufacturers and pellet mills.
[b] Sources: Keegan and White 1979; Keegan et al. 1979; McLain 1987; Miller and Wilson 1959; Morgan et al. 2005.

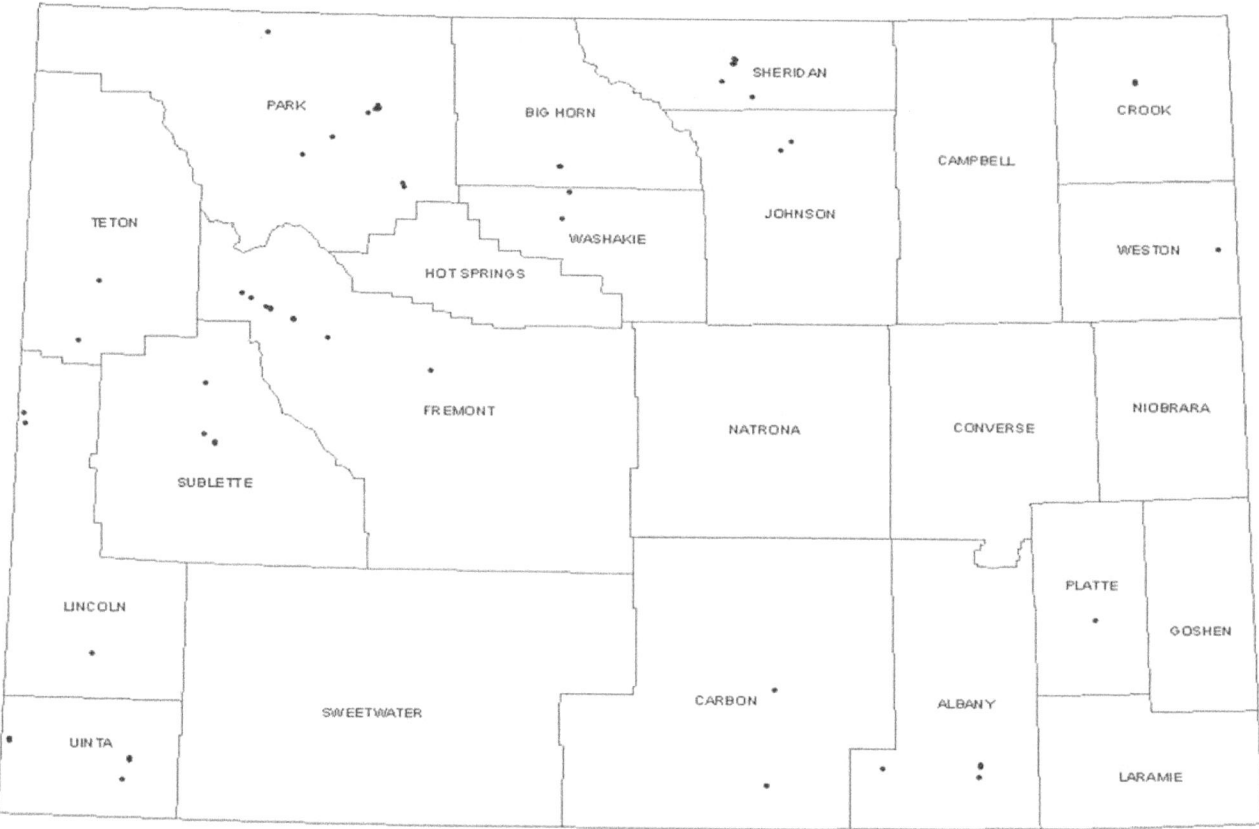

Figure 2—Location of Wyoming's active primary forest products manufacturers, 2005.

Timber-Processing Sectors

Sawmill Sector

Wyoming's 21 sawmills produced about 127 million board feet (MMBF) of lumber, timbers, and other sawn products in 2005. This was an increase of about 6 percent from the previous year's production of 114 MMBF (fig. 3). Since 2003 Wyoming's lumber production has actually been less than it was in the severe recession of 1982, when only 135 MMBF were produced (WWPA 1964-2006). Of the 127 MMBF produced in 2005, approximately 113 MMBF were lumber, while 14 MMBF were structural timbers and mine props.

Throughout the last 50 years, the number of sawmills in Wyoming has decreased and Wyoming's annual lumber production has fluctuated widely. However, the average output per mill has generally increased until the 2005 study, when average annual per-mill lumber production dropped by 18 percent (table 12). The 107 active sawmills identified by Miller and Wilson (1959) in 1957 had an average annual lumber production of 1.0 MMBF; the 50 active mills in 1976 had an average production of 4.1 MMBF (Keegan and White 1979; Keegan et al. 1979); the 23 sawmills active in 2000 produced an average of 7.3 MMBF (Morgan et al. 2005); and in 2005 the 21 facilities produced an average of 6.0 MMBF of lumber each.

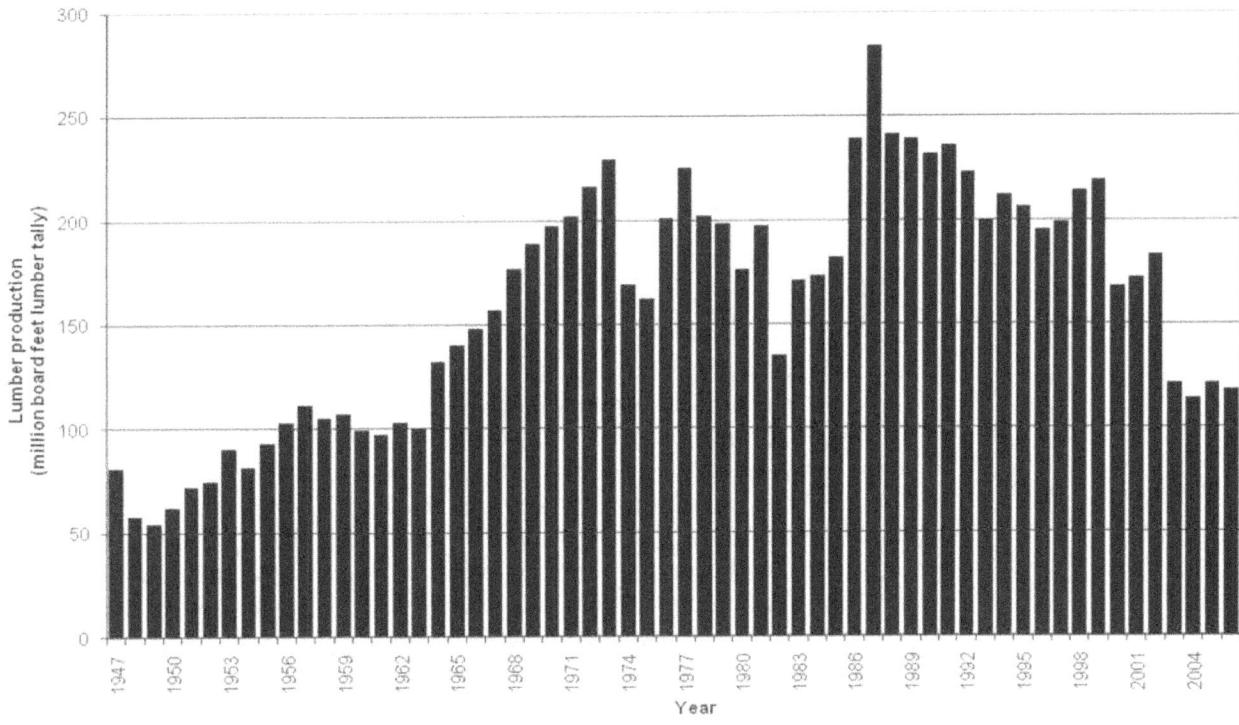

Figure 3—Wyoming lumber production, 1947-2006.

Table 12—Number of active Wyoming sawmills and average annual lumber production.

Year	Number of mills	Average annual lumber production
		million board feet, lumber tally
1957	107	1.0
1962	76	1.4
1966	65	1.9
1969	50	3.8
1974	49	3.4
1976	50	4.1
1983	34	5.0
2000	23	7.3
2005	21	6.0

Sources: Keegan and White 1979; Keegan et al. 1979; McLain 1987; Miller and Wilson 1959; Morgan et al. 2005; Setzer and Wilson 1970; Setzer 1971; Spencer and Farrenkopf 1964.

As in previous years, production in 2005 was concentrated in the state's largest mills. Four sawmills accounted for 89 percent of Wyoming's lumber production in 2005, whereas during 2000 the four largest mills accounted for 77 percent of Wyoming's lumber production (Morgan et al. 2005) (table 13). These four sawmills produced an average of 28.2 MMBF each. Six mills producing 1 MMBF to 10 MMBF accounted for 10 percent of Wyoming's 2005 production, and averaged 2.1 MMBF of annual lumber production. Eleven mills producing less than 1 MMBF accounted for the remaining 1 percent of statewide production.

Sawmills reported their annual output capacity in board feet lumber tally. Wyoming's 21 sawmills had about 177 MMBF of output capacity and utilized about 72 percent of capacity in 2005. This is in stark contrast to the 2000 report by Morgan et al. (2005) in which the 23 sawmills had about 376 MMBF of output capacity and only 45 percent of this capacity was utilized, which is well below the normal operating level of sawmills. The underutilization in 2000 was heavily influenced by two of the largest mills in the state that operated at a very low percentage of capacity and closed permanently in 2001 and 2003. In 2005, four mills with an annual output capacity greater than 10 MMBF accounted for 88 percent of the total estimated capacity. Six mills with capacity between 1 MMBF and 10 MMBF accounted for 10 percent of the total capacity, while the remaining 11 mills with capacity of 1 MMBF or less accounted for just 2 percent of Wyoming's estimated total capacity.

Wyoming's inflation-adjusted lumber sales for recent years are among the lowest on record (fig. 4). The lowest sales value, expressed in 2005 dollars, occurred in 2003 when sales only totaled about $37 million. In 2005, Wyoming's sales value had climbed to just over $46 million, which is still well below the sales value seen in the recession of the early 1980s. In 1982 Wyoming's lumber sales in constant 2005 dollars was about $55 million. From 1982 sales increased to the near record levels of approximately $126 million in 1994, after which the sales value dropped to about $100 million and remained relatively stable through 1999. Then in 2000, sales dropped sharply to around $60 million, where they remained until the 2003 low point. From 2003 to 2005 sales picked up slowly, going from $37 to $46 million and by 2006 sales had decreased to just under $42 million.

Overrun—the volume of lumber recovered from a board foot (Scribner) of timber— was calculated for each sawmill using timber processed and lumber production volumes. On average, Wyoming sawmills produced approximately 1.54 board feet of lumber for every board foot Scribner of timber processed, for a volume weighted average overrun of 54 percent in 2005. Overrun ranged from 25 to 95 percent among Wyoming's sawmills. Sawmills producing primarily random length dimension lumber and studs typically had greater overrun, and mills producing mostly boards and timbers had lower overrun. This is a dramatic improvement from 1976, when average overrun was only 18 percent. Over the last three decades, the increases in overrun have been due primarily to advances in milling technology and decreases in log diameter. As log diameter decreases, the Scribner Decimal C log rule, which is used in Wyoming, underestimates by an increasing amount the lumber that can be recovered, thus giving a higher lumber recovery per board foot Scribner of timber. Advances in production technology increase lumber recovery through computerized log sensing capabilities that identify optimum sawing patterns. Likewise, using thinner kerf saws and scanning equipment to edge and trim lumber has reduced the portion of the log that becomes sawdust.

Log Home Sector

Wyoming's log home industry has experienced substantial growth since 1976 when there were just four log home plants. By 2000, there were 11 facilities producing house logs or log homes, and in 2005 there were 18 log home facilities in Wyoming. Facilities in Wyoming's log home industry manufacture both house logs and complete log homes, and the industry offers two log styles: hand-hewn and sawn logs. Most firms specialize

Table 13—Number of active Wyoming sawmills by capacity size class, percentage of total capacity, production, and percentage of total production, 2005.

Lumber production capacity size class	Number of mills	Capacity	Percentage of total capacity	Average capacity per mill	Production	Percentage of total production	Average production per mill
		MBF [a]		MBF [a]	MBF [a]		MBF [a]
1 MMBF or less	11	4,735	2	430	1,910	1	174
Over 1 to 10 MMBF	6	17,200	10	2,867	12,351	10	2,059
Over 10 MMBF	4	154,820	88	38,705	112,696	89	28,174
Total	21	176,755	100	8,417	126,957	100	6,046

[a] Production and capacity expressed in thousand board feet (MBF) lumber tally.

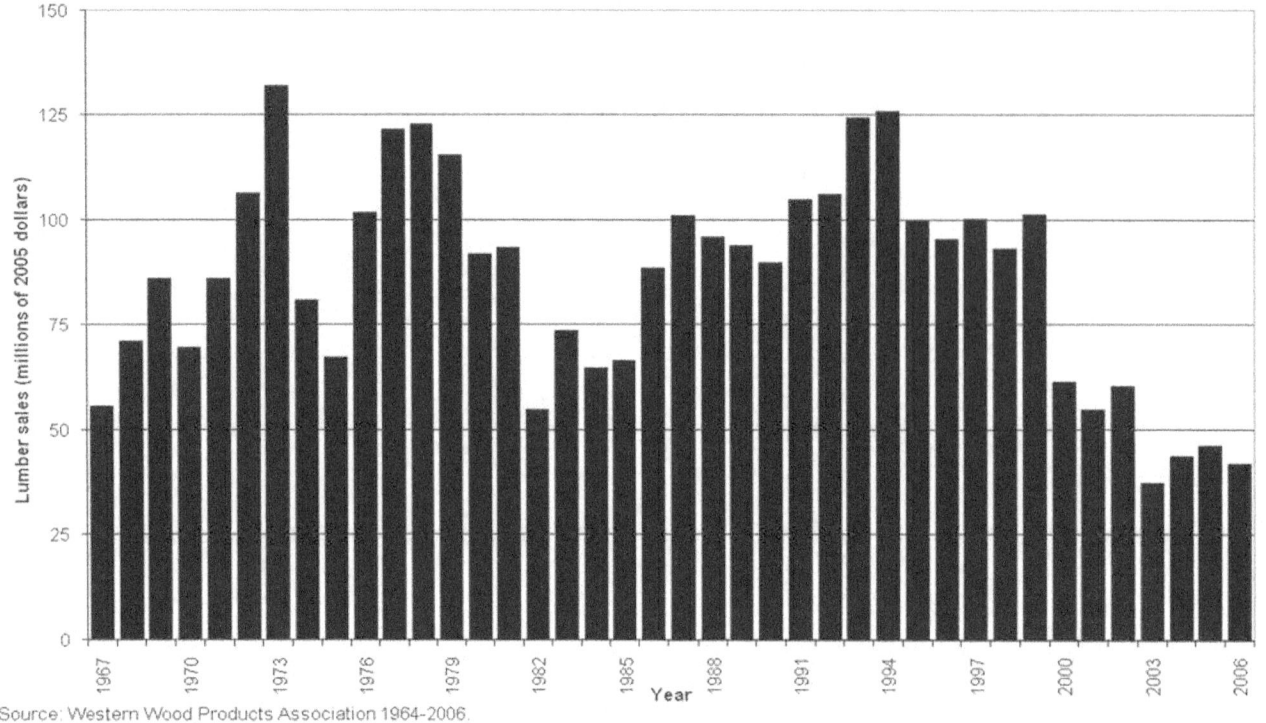

Source: Western Wood Products Association 1964-2006.

Figure 4—Wyoming lumber sales, 1967-2006.

in one of the two styles. In 2005, Wyoming's house log and log home manufacturers had sales of about $9.2 million, selling 557 thousand lineal feet (MLF) of house logs. Forty-four percent of sales were sawn logs and 56 percent were hand-hewn. The 2005 sales value represents a 16 percent increase from $7.9 million (2005 dollars) in 2000, but the volume of house logs sold decreased 33 percent from the 830 MLF sold in 2000. The increase in sales value in conjunction with a decrease of the volume of house logs sold is due primarily to there being a larger proportion of hand peeled house logs sold in 2005. During 2000, only 20 percent of the house logs sold were hand peeled, while nearly 75 percent of the manufactured house logs were sawn. In 2005 more than half the house logs sold were hand peeled. Hand peeled logs command a much higher price, often two to three times as much as logs that are sawn or machine turned. In 1976, production and sales data on the log home sector were combined with data from other sectors of Wyoming's timber processing industry to protect firm-level data (Keegan and White 1979). Sales for those combined sectors totaled $8 million in 1976, slightly less than half of the combined sales for 2005.

Log Furniture Sector

Wyoming's log furniture sector has grown over the past 30 years. In 1976, no firms producing log furniture were reported; by 2000 there were 11 firms operating, and in 2005 there were only 8 facilities. Even though the number of firms producing log furniture decreased, the total sales value increased slightly from $1.2 million (2005 dollars) in 2000 to $1.5 million in 2005. This sector predominately uses small-diameter (less than 7 inches d.b.h.) lodgepole pine timber to construct log furniture. The logs are typically debarked and assembled into different types of furniture including bed frames, chairs, tables, and couch frames.

Other Sectors

Other sectors of Wyoming's primary forest products industry include post and pole producers, wood pellet plants, and a commercial firewood cutter. Combined sales values for these sectors were $7.8 million in 2005. Eight of the 12 facilities in this sector produced posts and poles, three were fuel pellet producers that utilized mill residues, and one was a commercial firewood cutter. Eight post and pole facilities along with five firewood and wood pellet plants were identified in 2000 (Morgan et al. 2005). Going back to 1976, seven post and pole facilities were in operation, while only one plant produced other products (Keegan and White 1979). Production statistics and sales figures for these individual sectors are not provided in order to protect firm-level data.

Capacity to Process Timber

Respondent mills were asked to specify their shift and annual product output capacities (production capacity), assuming sufficient supplies of raw materials and a firm market demand for their products. Input capacity was then calculated for each facility, using the mill's stated production capacity and recovery (e.g., overrun). The estimate of capacity to process timber or "timber-processing capacity" is expressed in units of timber input (i.e., board feet Scribner). Wyoming's total estimated capacity to process timber in 2005 was 132 MMBF Scribner (table 14). However, only 67 percent of this capacity was utilized, with almost 89 MMBF of timber being processed in 2005. By comparison, Wyoming's total estimated capacity to process timber in 2000 was nearly twice as much (260 MMBF), with just 44 percent (114 MMBF) utilized.

Wyoming's capacity to process timber has been declining for nearly two decades, with the loss of 176 MMBF or 57 percent of the state's ability to process timber between 1986 and 2005. The largest capacity loss occurred between 2000 and 2005, when timber-processing capacity dropped nearly 128 MMBF Scribner. This was largely due to the closure of two of Wyoming's major sawmills: the mill in New Castle and the mill in Saratoga.

Sawmills accounted for 86 percent (114 MMBF) of Wyoming's total timber-processing capacity in 2005. The state's four largest sawmills had timber-processing capacity of 98 MMBF, accounting for 86 percent of sawmill capacity. The four largest mills also processed 87 percent (72 MMBF) of the timber used by sawmills in Wyoming (table 15).

Table 14—Wyoming's timber processing capacity and volume utilized, 1976-2005.

Year	Processing capacity	Volume utilized	Percent utilized
	- - - - - - - MBF[a] - - - - - -		
1976	302,083	147,280	49
1983	272,867	153,260	56
1986	307,800	153,608	50
1996	273,483	116,906	43
2000	260,194	113,687	44
2002	217,094	74,875	34
2005	132,285	88,522	67

[a] Timber processing capacity and volume utilized expressed in thousand board feet (MBF) Scr bner.

Sources: Keegan and White 1979; Keegan et al. 1979; McLain 1987; Morgan et al. 2005.

Table 15—Number of active Wyoming sawmills by capacity size class, percentage of total timber use, timber use, and percentage of total timber use, 2005.

Lumber production capacity size class[a]	Number of mills	Timber capacity	Percentage of total timber capacity	Average timber capacity per mill	Timber use	Percentage of total timber use	Average timber use per mill
		MBF[b]		*MBF[b]*	*MBF[b]*		*MBF[b]*
1 MMBF or less	11	3,513	3	319	1,492	2	136
Over 1 to 10 MMBF	6	12,532	11	2,089	9,254	11	1,542
Over 10 MMBF	4	98,217	86	24,554	71,710	87	17,928
Total	21	114,263	100	5,441	82,456	100	3,926

[a] Lumber production capacity expressed in million board feet (MMBF) lumber tally.
[b] Timber use and capacity expressed in thousand board feet (MBF) Scr bner.

Eleven percent (12 MMBF) of sawmill timber-processing capacity was held by the six mid-size sawmills that processed just over 9 MMBF (11 percent) of the timber received by Wyoming sawmills. The remaining three percent (4 MMBF) of sawmill capacity was spread among the 11 smaller sawmills in the state that processed just two percent (1 MMBF) of the timber utilized by sawmills.

Log Utilization and Mill Residue

This section traces the flow of Wyoming's timber harvest through various manufacturing sectors. Since mill residues as well as timber and finished products are accounted for, volumes are presented in cubic feet. The following conversion factors, developed from the 2005 census of timber processors, were used to convert board foot Scribner volume to cubic feet of bole wood:

- 5.00 board feet per cubic foot for house logs
- 4.78 board feet per cubic foot for sawlogs
- 3.19 board feet per cubic foot for other timber products

Log Utilization

Wyoming's timber harvest in 2005 was approximately 13,674 thousand cubic feet (MCF), exclusive of bark (fig. 5). Of this volume, 92.5 percent went as logs to sawmills, 6.8 percent went to post and pole plants, log furniture plants, and other facilities, and just under 1 percent went to log home manufacturers. Sawmills received 12,650 MCF logs, producing 6,008 MCF of finished lumber, while 6,433 MCF (51 percent) of volume delivered to sawmills became mill residue. Nearly all the residue (6,424 MCF) generated from sawmills was shipped to other facilities to be utilized as fuel or processed into another product. Only 9 MCF of the residue generated from sawmills was not used, and 209 MCF was lost to shrinkage while drying lumber.

House log and log home manufacturers received 98 MCF of timber from Wyoming's timberlands in 2005. Approximately 56 MCF became finished goods, and 42 MCF became residue. Other facilities, including post and pole plants, log furniture producers, and wood pellet manufacturers received about 926 MCF of Wyoming wood fiber in 2005. About 276 MCF of this material became residue, with 235 MCF being used in other products and 41 MCF going unused.

Mill Residue Quantity, Type, and Use

As indicated above, a substantial portion, about 51 percent, of the wood fiber processed by primary forest products plants ends up as mill residue. Mill residue from primary wood products manufacturers can present difficult and expensive disposal problems, or they can be used to produce additional products and generate revenue. Three types of wood residues are typically created by Wyoming's primary wood products industry: coarse residue, consisting of slabs, edging, trim, and log ends; fine residue, consisting primarily of planer shavings and sawdust; and bark. The 2005 census gathered information on volumes and uses of mill residue. Actual residue volumes were obtained from facilities that sold all or most of their residues, and all mills reported, on a percent basis, how their residues were used. The peelings from the log home, log furniture, and the post and pole facilities are included with the coarse residue.

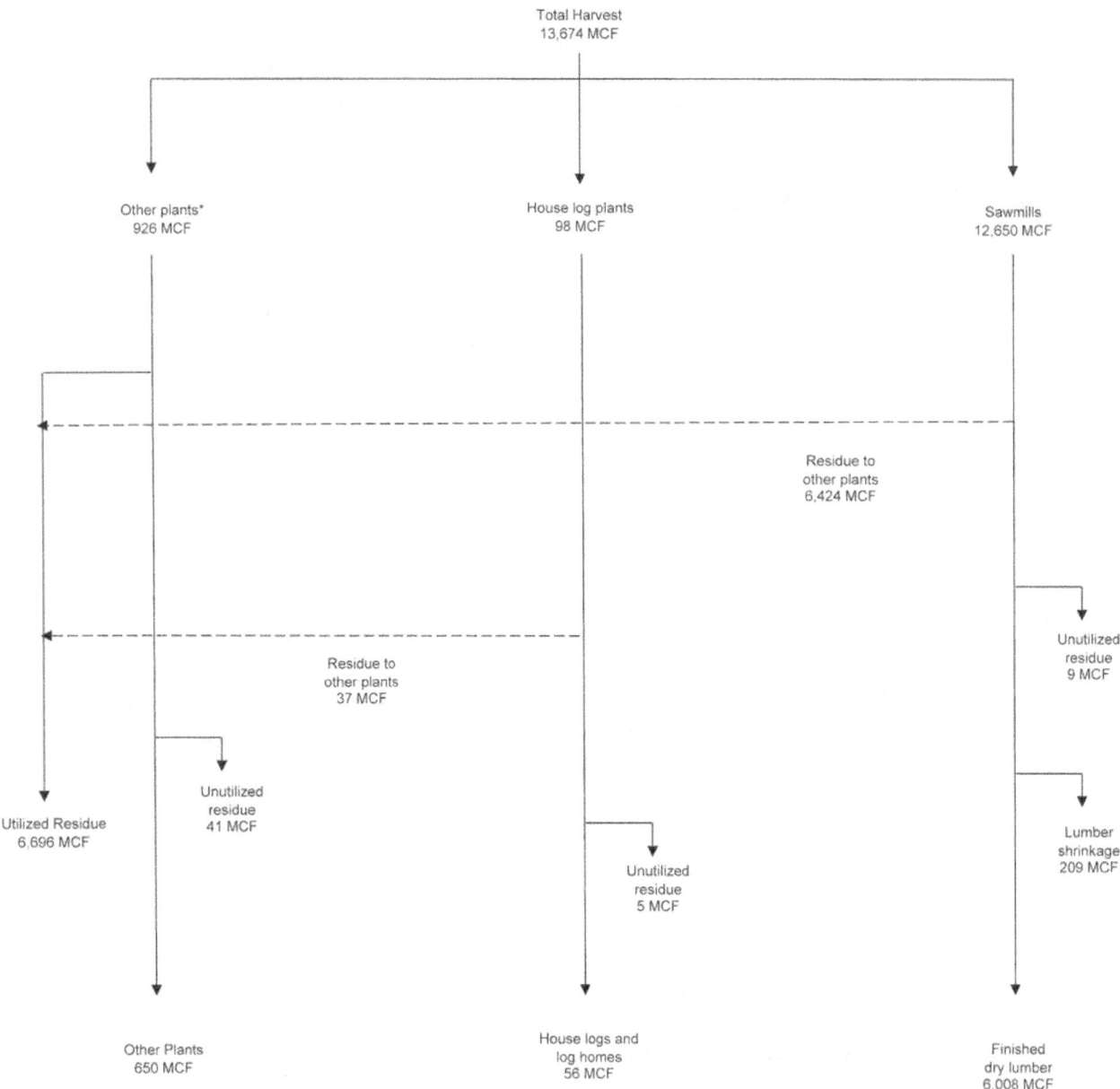

Total Harvest
13,674 MCF

Other plants*
926 MCF

House log plants
98 MCF

Sawmills
12,650 MCF

Residue to
other plants
6,424 MCF

Unutilized
residue
9 MCF

Residue to
other plants
37 MCF

Unutilized
residue
41 MCF

Utilized Residue
6,696 MCF

Unutilized
residue
5 MCF

Lumber
shrinkage
209 MCF

Other Plants
650 MCF

House logs and
log homes
56 MCF

Finished
dry lumber
6,008 MCF

* Other plants include wood pellet manufacturers and out-of-state
pulp and reconstituted board plants.

Figure 5—Wyoming timber harvest and flow, 2005.

Statewide residue volume factors (table 16), which express mill residue generated per MBF of lumber produced, were derived from production and residue output volumes provided by sawmills. Sawmills accounted for 95.8 percent of all mill residues generated in Wyoming in 2005. Sawmills generated more than 120,500 bone dry units (BDU) of mill residue; 92 percent of this residue was utilized (table 17). One bone dry unit is the equivalent of 2,400 pounds of ovendry wood.

Facilities other than sawmills produced about 5,200 BDU of residue, meaning all Wyoming timber processors generated about 125,000 BDU of residue in 2005. The proportion of Wyoming's mill residues that are utilized has been increasing since the late 1960s. For all residue combined, utilization has increased from 33 percent in 1969, to 60 percent in 1983, 85 percent in 2000, and 92 percent in 2005 (table 18).

Coarse residue was the state's largest wood products residue component (41 percent of all residues) in 2005. Wyoming's primary wood products facilities produced nearly 52,000 BDU of coarse residue, of which less than 800 BDU (1.5 percent) were unused (table 19). Nearly 79 percent of coarse residue were chipped and sold out-of-state to pulp and paper mills and reconstituted board plants, 13 percent were burned as fuel, and about 8 percent were sold and used for other products.

Approximately 99 percent of both coarse and fine residues were utilized in 2005, which is on par with utilization levels in 2000. This high level of mill residue utilization represents a significant increase, especially for fine residue, since the 1960s and 1970s. This residue utilization increase is likely due to pulp mills expanding and higher energy costs increasing the demand for wood for energy, such as wood pellets. Historically, more than half of Wyoming's coarse residues have been utilized, whereas less than half of fines were utilized. Fine residue made up the second largest component (34 percent)

Table 16—Wyoming's 2005 sawmill residue factors.

Type of residue	Bone-dry units [a]
	per thousand board feet lumber tally
Coarse	0.38
Sawdust	0.24
Planer Shavings	0.09
Bark	0.25
Total	0.96

[a] Bone-dry units (2,400 lbs. of ovendry wood) of the various residue types generated for every 1,000 board feet of lumber manufactured.

Table 17—Estimated volume of wood residue generated and utilized by Wyoming's sawmills, 2005.

Residue type	Wood residue			Percentage of type		
	Used	Unused	Total	Used	Unused	Total
	- - - - - - Bone-dry units- - - - - -			- - - - - - - - Percent - - - - - - - - -		
Coarse	47,762	4	47,766	100.0	0.0	40
Fine a	41,066	119	41,185	99.7	0.3	34
Bark	21,994	9,566	31,560	69.7	30.3	26
Total	110,822	9,689	120,511	92.0	8.0	100

[a] Fine residue includes sawdust and planer shavings.

Table 18—Historical utilization of Wyoming mill residues.

Residue	Year	Used	Unused
		--- Percent ---	
Coarse	2005	98.5	1.5
	2000	97.7	2.3
	1983	77.4	22.6
	1976	77.8	22.2
	1969	58.2	41.8
Fine	2005	99.7	0.3
	2000	98.8	1.2
	1983	49.4	50.6
	1976	34.9	65.1
	1969	28.7	71.3
Bark	2005	69.8	30.2
	2000	32.5	67.5
	1983	31.9	68.1
	1976	11.7	88.3
	1969	0.1	99.9
All residues	2005	91.9	8.1
	2000	84.5	15.5
	1983	59.5	40.5
	1976	48.6	51.4
	1969	32.8	67.2

Sources: Keegan and White 1979; Keegan et al. 1979; McLain 1987; Morgan et al. 2005; Setzer 1971.

Table 19—Wyoming's production and disposition of residues, 2005.

Type of residue	Total utilized	Reconstituted products	Hogfuel	Other uses	Unused	Total
			- Bone-dry units -			
Coarse[a]	51,127	40,323	6,443	4,261	774	51,901
Fine:						
Sawdust	29,586	1,822	7,635	20,129	119	29,705
Planer shavings	12,482	1,320	—	11,162	—	12,482
Bark	22,105	—	15,886	6,219	9,566	31,671
Total	115,300	43,465	29,964	41,771	10,459	125,759

[a] Includes residue from the manufacture of post and poles, house logs, and log furniture, as well as lumber and plywood.

of residue in 2005, at just over 42,000 BDU. Sawdust comprised 70 percent and planer shavings 30 percent of fine residue. Less than 1 percent (119 BDU) of the fine residue were left unused with the major uses for fine residues being fuel (7,600 BDU), reconstituted products (3,100 BDU), and wood pellets and other uses (31,300 BDU).

Bark, which has typically been the least utilized residue, has undergone dramatic increases in utilization since 1969, when less than 1 percent was utilized. From 1983 to 2000, bark utilization remained rather consistent at about 32 percent, while in 2005 approximately 70 percent of the bark was used. Of the roughly 32,000 BDUs of bark produced by Wyoming facilities, 50 percent (15,900 BDU) was burned for fuel, 20 percent (6,200 BDU) was used in other products, and the remaining 30 percent (9,600 BDU) was not used.

Product Markets, Employment, and Labor Income

Products, Markets, and Sales Value

Mills summarized their 2005 shipments of finished wood products, providing information on volume, sales value, and geographic destination. Mills usually distributed their products in two ways: through their own distribution channels, or through independent wholesalers and selling agents. Because of subsequent wholesaling transactions, the geographic destination reported here may not precisely reflect final delivery points of shipments.

The estimated total sales value of Wyoming's primary forest products in 2005 was nearly $76 million free on board (f.o.b.) the producing mill (table 20). The North Central and Rocky Mountain States (including Wyoming) collectively accounted for more than 80 percent of Wyoming's total primary wood products sales. Wyoming purchasers were responsible for approximately 21 percent of the total wood products sales. Wyoming lumber purchasers accounted for nearly 10 percent of lumber sales in 2005. Roughly 68 percent of house logs and log homes were sold in Wyoming, while approximately 15 percent were sold in other Rocky Mountain States, making those two areas responsible for 83 percent of the sales of house logs and log homes. This sales distribution was substantially different than in 2000, when the Rocky Mountain States accounted for approximately 44 percent of the sales of house logs and log homes, while Wyoming accounted for roughly 20 percent and the North Central and Southern States were responsible for approximately 15 percent each. The shift in sales was likely due to increased building in Wyoming. The majority (72 percent) of other primary products stayed within Wyoming and the Rocky Mountain States, which accounted for 43 and 29 percent of sales respectively.

Table 20—Destination and value of Wyoming's 2005 primary wood products sales.

Product	Wyoming	Rocky Mountains[a]	Far West[b]	North Central[c]	Northeast[d]	South[e]	Other areas[f]	Total
				-Thousands of dollars -				
Lumber, timbers, and associated products	5,864	15,141	1,544	26,419	591	9,224	—	58,784
House logs and log houses	6,291	1,382	979	270	—	309	—	9,231
Other primary wood products[g]	3,416	2,262	1,074	758	115	139	108	7,872
All primary wood products	15,571	18,785	3,597	27,447	706	9,673	108	75,887
				Percentage of sales -				
Lumber, timbers, and associated products	7.7	20.0	2.0	34.8	0.8	12.2	—	77.5
House logs and log houses	8.3	1.8	1.3	0.4	—	0.4	—	12.2
Other primary wood products[g]	4.5	3.0	1.4	1.0	0.2	0.2	0.1	10.4
All primary wood products	20.5	24.8	4.7	36.2	0.9	12.7	0.1	100

[a] Rocky Mountains includes Arizona, Colorado, Idaho, Montana, Nevada, New Mexico, and Utah.
[b] Far West includes Alaska, California, Hawaii, Oregon, and Washington.
[c] North Central includes Illinois, Indiana, Iowa, Kansas, Michigan, Minnesota, Missouri, Nebraska, North Dakota, Ohio, South Dakota, and Wisconsin.
[d] Northeast includes Connecticut, Maine, Massachusetts, New Hampshire, New Jersey, New York, Pennsylvania, Rhode Island, and Vermont.
[e] South includes Alabama, Arkansas, Delaware, Florida, Georgia, Kentucky, Louisiana, Maryland, Mississippi, North Carolina, Oklahoma, South Carolina, Tennessee, Texas, Virginia, and West Virginia.
[f] Other areas consist of products being shipped outside the United States.
[g] Other products include posts, poles, other roundwood products, wood pellets, and firewood.

USDA Forest Service Resour. Bull. RMRS-RB-9. 2009

25

Employment and Labor Income

This section discusses trends in employment and labor income from 1990 through 2006 in Wyoming's forest products industry. Employment data developed as part of the FIDACS census were used in conjunction with employment and earnings data from the U.S. Department of Commerce, Regional Economic Information System (REIS) and the U.S. Census Bureau's County Business Patterns to identify employment for Wyoming's primary and secondary forest products industry (U.S. Census Bureau 2008; U.S. Department of Commerce 2008). The primary forest products industry includes logging, processing logs into lumber and other wood products, processing wood fiber residue from timber processors, and private sector forest management services. The secondary industry includes firms processing outputs from the primary industry, although the outputs may be from mills in Wyoming or elsewhere. Secondary products include outputs like prefabricated buildings, trusses, moulding, millwork and cut stock, doors, and windows.

The REIS system uses the North American Industry Classification System (NAICS) as defined by the U.S. Office of Management and Budget to report on industry sectors. The primary and secondary forest products industry sectors are captured in two categories (OMB 1998): NAICS 113 (forestry and logging) and NAICS 321 (wood product manufacturing). These industrial classifications give a conservative representation of forest industry employment and labor income; however, the correspondence is not exact. A number of activities involving workers associated with forest products such as truck or rail transport of logs, wood fiber, or finished products, and timber product management activities by government employees are not included.

In 2006, the most recent year for which comprehensive information is available, there were 1,354 workers in Wyoming's forest products industry and these workers earned approximately $41 million in labor income or workers earnings. Labor income includes wages, some benefits, and earnings of the self-employed. Of the 1,354 workers, approximately 250 were employed in logging and other private sector forest management activities, just over 650 were employed in processing timber, and the remaining 440 workers were involved in secondary processing of lumber and other primary wood products.

Since 1990, total employment in Wyoming's forest products industry has declined by more than 20 percent or roughly 400 workers (fig. 6). The decline has been concentrated in the logging and timber processing sectors with the secondary component increasing slightly (30 workers) from 1990 to 2006. The major reason for the decline in Wyoming's forest products industry employment over this time period was the decline in timber harvest, particularly from federal lands, in Wyoming and adjacent states.

Total inflation-adjusted labor income in constant 2005 dollars in Wyoming's forest products industry has decreased by 23 percent since 1990 (fig. 7) from nearly $53 million to $41 million in 2006. Similar to employment, the decrease in labor income was in the primary timber harvesting and processing components with growth in the secondary wood products industry. Labor income in the forestry and logging sectors declined by more than 50 percent from nearly $16 million in 1990 to just over $7 million in 2006; labor income in the timber processing component declined from $41 to $27 million (34 percent). Labor income in Wyoming's secondary industry increased from $11 million dollars in 1990 to $13 million in 2006.

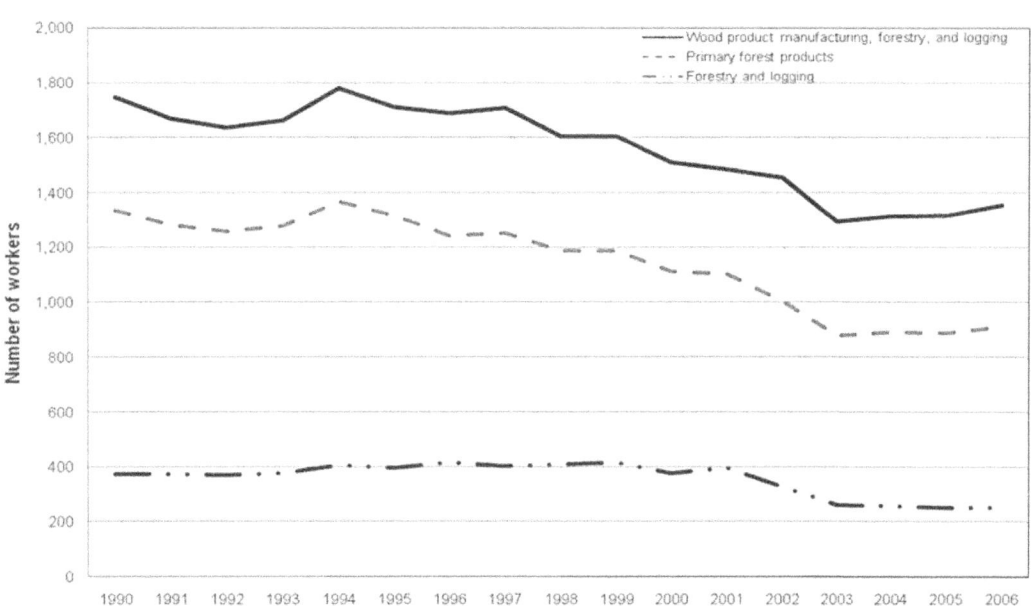

Figure 6—Employment in Wyoming's forest products industry, 1990-2006.

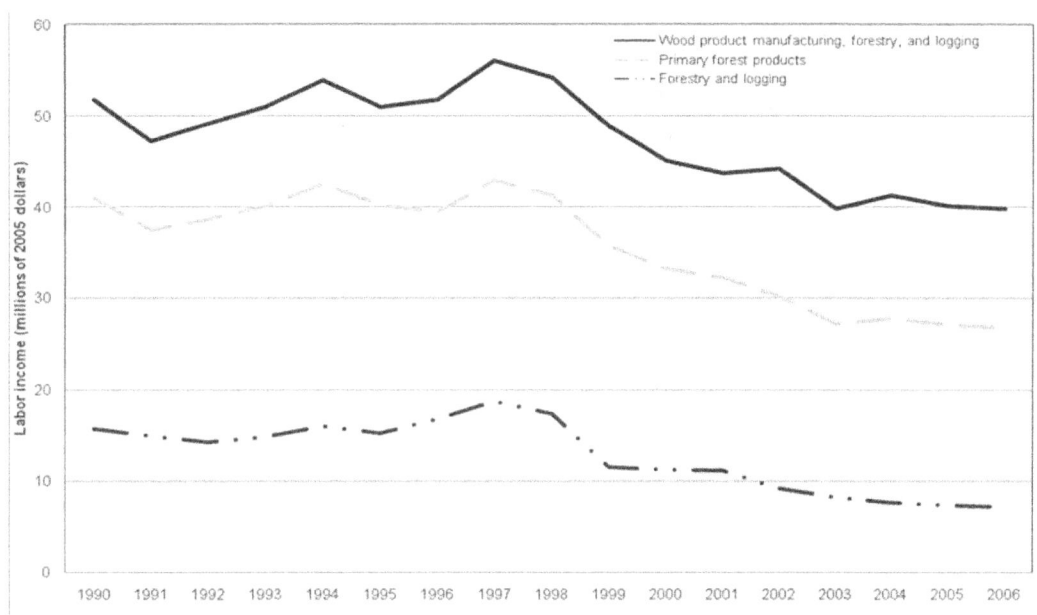

Figure 7—Labor income in Wyoming's forest products industry, 1990-2006.

USDA Forest Service Resour. Bull. RMRS-RB-9. 2009

27

References

Bechtold, W.A., and P.L. Patterson, eds. 2005. The enhanced Forest Inventory and Analysis program—national sampling design and estimation procedures. Gen. Tech. Rep. SRS-80. Asheville, NC: U.S. Department of Agriculture, Forest Service, Southern Research Station. 85 p.

Green, A.W.; Conner, R.C. 1989. Forests in Wyoming. Resour. Bull. INT-61. Ogden, UT: U.S. Department of Agriculture, Forest Service, Intermountain Research Station. 91 p.

Johnson, T.G., ed. 2001. United States timber industry—an assessment of timber product output and use, 1996. Gen. Tech. Rep. SRS-45. Asheville, NC: U.S. Department of Agriculture, Forest Service, Southern Research Station. 145 p.

Keegan, C.E., T.A. Morgan, K.M. Gebert, J.P. Brandt, K.A. Blatner and T.P. Spoelma. 2006. Timber-processing capacity and capabilities in the Western United States. Journal of Forestry 104 (5): 262-268.

Keegan, C.E. and R.V. White. 1979. Wyoming forest products industry. Institute for Policy Research, University of Wyoming. Wyoming Issues 2:(4)2-7.

Keegan, C.E., R.V. White, and T.S. Setzer. 1979. Wyoming timber production and mill residues—1976. Resour. Bull. INT-19. Ogden, UT: U.S. Department of Agriculture, Forest Service, Intermountain Forest and Range Experiment Station. 5 p.

McLain, W.H. 1987. Wyoming and western South Dakota's 1983 fuelwood harvest. Resour. Bull. INT-47. Ogden, UT: U.S. Department of Agriculture, Forest Service, Intermountain Research Station. 10 p.

McLain, W.H. 1988. Logging utilization—Colorado, Wyoming, and western South Dakota. Resour. Bull. INT-52. Ogden, UT: U.S. Department of Agriculture, Forest Service, Intermountain Research Station. 10 p.

Miller, R.L., and A.K. Wilson. 1959. Lumber production in Wyoming, 1957. Survey Release 2. Ogden, UT: U.S. Department of Agriculture, Forest Service, Rocky Mountain Forest and Range Experiment Station. 9 p.

Morgan, T.A., T.P. Spoelma, C.E. Keegan, A.L. Chase and M.T. Thompson. 2005. Wyoming's forest products industry and timber harvest, 2000. Resour. Bull. RMRS-RB-5. Fort Collins, CO: U.S. Department of Agriculture, Forest Service, Rocky Mountain Research Station. 25 p.

Office of Management and Budget [OMB]. 1987. Standard industrial classification manual. Springfield, VA: Executive Office of the President. 705 p.

Office of Management and Budget [OMB]. 1998. North American industrial classification system. Lanham, MD: Executive Office of the President. 1247 p.

RISI. 2007. 2007 Lockwood-Post directory of pulp and paper mills: The Americas (traveler's edition). Boston, MA. 541 p.

Random Lengths. 2006. Big book 2006: the buyers and sellers directory of the forest products industry. Eugene, OR. 1168 p.

Setzer, T.S. 1971. Estimates of timber products output and plant residues, Wyoming and western South Dakota, 1969. Res. Note INT-136. Ogden, UT: U.S. Department of Agriculture, Forest Service, Intermountain Forest and Range Experiment Station. 6 p.

Setzer, T.S.; Wilson, A.K. 1970. Timber products in the Rocky Mountain States, 1966. Resour. Bull. INT-9. Ogden, UT: U.S. Department of Agriculture, Forest Service, Intermountain Forest and Range Experiment Station. 89 p.

Spencer, J.S., and T.O. Farrenkopf. 1964. Timber products output in Colorado, Wyoming, and western South Dakota, 1962. Res. Pap. INT-14. Ogden, UT: U.S. Department of Agriculture, Forest Service, Intermountain Forest and Range Experiment Station, 18 p.

Thompson, M.T., L.T. DeBlander and J.A. Blackard. 2005. Wyoming's Forests, 2002. Resour. Bull. RMRS-RB-6. Fort Collins, CO: U.S. Department of Agriculture, Forest Service, Rocky Mountain Research Station. 148 p.

U.S. Census Bureau. 2008. County Business Patterns [CBP]. Available online at http://www.census.gov/epcd/cbp/view/cbpview.html Last accessed April 2008.

U.S. Department of Commerce, Bureau of Economic Analysis [BEA]. 2008. Regional Economic Information System (REIS). Available online at www.bea.gov/regional/reis/ Last accessed April 2008.

Western Wood Products Association [WWPA]. 1964-2006. Statistical yearbook of the Western lumber industry. Portland, OR.